MODERN ORIENTAL CARPETS

A Buyer's Guide

By

Donald P. Schlick

Illustrations

by

Yvonne J. Schlick

Charles E. Tuttle Company
Rutland, Vermont & Tokyo, Japan

Representatives

For Continental Europe:
BOXERBOOKS, INC., Zurich

For the British Isles:
PRENTICE-HALL INTERNATIONAL, INC., London

For Australasia:
PAUL FLESCH & CO., PTY. LTD., Melbourne

For Canada:
M. G. HURTIG, LTD., Edmonton

Published by the Charles E. Tuttle Company, Inc.
of Rutland, Vermont & Tokyo, Japan
with editorial offices at
Suido 1-chome, 2-6, Bunkyo-ku, Tokyo

Library of Congress Catalog Card No. 72-123896
Standard Book No. 8048-0930-5

Printed in Hongkong

TABLE OF CONTENTS

ILLUSTRATIONS

ORIENTAL CARPET PLATES

ACKNOWLEDGEMENTS

Initial thanks go to Pat and Bob Ferraro for providing the stimulus to begin this book. Pat and Bob are talented authors themselves who painstakingly lent their editing skill to improve this manuscript. Ken Greiner, Rod Heller, and Munir Afredi also assisted by providing comments and critique when necessary.

Special acknowledgement goes to Glenn Malmberg, Win Mumby, Jim Calkins, Paul Garnett, Ivan Peterson, Norman French, and Tony Berkes who loaned their carpets to be photographed. Appreciation is also extended to the Pak-Punjab Carpet Factory, Lahore, West Pakistan; Peer Mohammad Din, Kabul, Afghanistan; and Cyrus Carpets and Far Carpets, Tehran, Iran, for sharing with the author their time and carpets.

A final word of appreciation is due my wife who contributed the numerous drawings and cover design which have helped so much to make this volume complete. Also I should not leave out my children, Doniece, Susan, and D.J., who all contributed by helping to compile the final draft.

PREFACE

The idea for this book has been with me for several years but was not brought to the forefront until a three month visit to the United States in November of 1966 and a subsequent boat trip from Karachi, West Pakistan, to Mombassa, Kenya, in August of 1967. Because we have lived in Pakistan for the last six years and have had the opportunity to leisurely study and examine carpets which we have always enjoyed, this book and it's purpose are finally being realized.

From the onset I intended this book to be a systematic economic survey of modern Oriental carpets rather than a detailed chronology of past events which are adequately covered by books listed in the bibliography. I have given considerable attention to Oriental carpet buying focussing on easily discernible factors and values. The formula and graph presented have frequently been put to the test in Iran, Pakistan, Afghanistan, and India from 1963 to 1968.

The initial chapters were written and later updated after visiting Tehran, Isphan, Shiraz, Kashan, and Qum in Iran and also Kabul, Afghanistan, in December 1967. These trips permitted me to take photographs of the newest design characteristics and patterns currently available on the market.

On my last trip to Tehran, my good friend John Ryan insisted I see the modern Persian carpet exhibition at the Decorative Arts Museum located at 227 Amerkabir Ave., Tehran, Iran. A complete collection of over 200 modern Persian carpets are permanently housed here and certainly worthwhile for any carpet collector or interested person who has the opportunity to visit Tehran.

D.P.S.
Lahore, West Pakistan
Feb. 1968

AN UNDERSTANDING OF CARPETS

An Oriental carpet is a hand knotted floor covering woven in one of seven Asian countries: Iran, Pakistan, Afghanistan, India, Turkey, Russia, or China. Turkey is the western boundary of the Oriental carpet world which extends to China on the east and Russia on the north. See Fig. 1.

Size often determines whether or not a floor covering is called a rug or a carpet. British phrasing denotes a rug to be under 40 square feet while a carpet is larger. In the United States a floor covering extending from wall to wall is a carpet, everything else is a rug. In this book, as in the Orient, the words are synonymous.

An antique Oriental carpet must be 100 years old in order to qualify under United States Customs regulations. Semi-antique has come to mean the rug must be 50 years old. A rug classified as an antique piece may be less serviceable than a newer rug no matter how mellow. However, many other considerations such as condition, color and design are necessary to determine intrinsic value.

The Eastern countries where the Oriental carpet originated have had a continuous, eventful, and colorful history. Individual countries have been conquered, invaded, destroyed, and reconquered. During these transitions many new and improved tools and luxuries desirable to mankind were invented and improved upon. The Oriental carpet has received characteristics from all these processes, but it is unique in that it survived all these years without any outstanding technical innovations. Today modern Oriental carpet weaving methods, material characteristics, and pattern designs have not appreciably changed since the days of Akbar the Great who was responsible for importing Persian weavers into the Indian sub-continent.

Despite an early origin, Oriental rugs did not enter the American scene until the late 1800's. Almost at once they became prized possessions resulting in a short supply during the early 1900's. Weavers were kept busy until the Great Depression created a sharp decline in purchasing power. However, as the Western world repaired the damage of the depression, Oriental rugs were again imported. The growing demand for woven carpets directly relates to the general prosperity of the Free World in the wake of World War II.

12

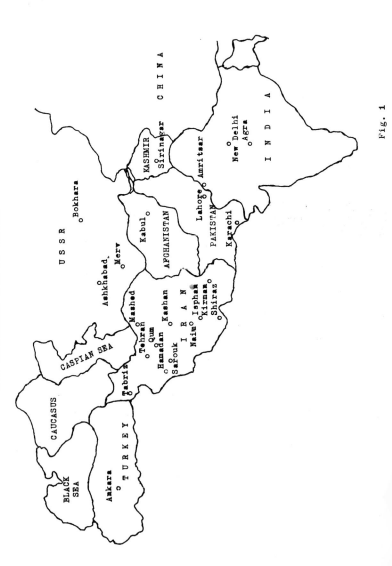

THE ORIENTAL CARPET WORLD

Fig. 1

Early rug retailers in the U.S. learned that prospective American buyers were not interested in the naturally bright colors of Oriental rugs. Rather than bold colors, the Americans were interested in subdued tones bordering on pastel shades. The American businessman, not to be denied a place in this lucrative business, devised a unique system of chemically washing the carpets to reduce the intensity of the bright colors, thus making them palatable to the American eye. However, loss in carpet life was sacrificed for quieter colors. A chemical wash damages the protein in the wool fibers causing them to become brittle and easily broken. Most of the rugs imported into the United States during the early 1920's were, in some degree, chemically washed, and it wasn't until the mid 1950's that a compromise was accepted which favored less bold color tones and light chemical treatments.

During the late 1950's and early 1960's a shortage in the supply of Oriental carpets was created by Iranians, Americans, and Europeans purchasing more carpets than existing looms were capable of weaving. As a result the Oriental carpet became an investment and a hedge against inflation.

Today Iran is by far the most important rug weaving area. Persian carpets are in great demand in Europe and the United States.

Turkoman, Pakistani, and Indian carpets are also gaining popularity in the foreign markets perhaps on a larger scale than Persian carpets. Some Oriental rug experts suggest that India will dominate the future international carpet weaving industry, primarily because of the number of rugs produced in India. Indian carpets are sought after in the United States; however, London is the principal market for Indian rugs. Turkoman carpets are in great demand in West Germany.

A projection should be attempted to give the prospective Oriental rug purchaser an indication of future values. Many Oriental carpet enthusiasts believe that carpet weaving will become extinct in the future. This alarming statement is predicated on the rationale that wages are increasing in the carpet weaving areas and that no technical innovations have been introduced to help reduce labor costs; consequently, prices of Oriental carpets are rising. On the demand side, the propensity of rug buying increases as individuals satisfy basic consumption needs which releases additional money for luxury items. Therefore one can conclude that although the prices of Oriental carpets are rising, buyers are becoming more affluent and can afford to pay more. Figures recently published in the November 1967 issue of "FRONT LINES", the United States Agency for International Development publication, indicate that the export of Persian carpets is increasing. The article states, "Progress in Iran has not replaced the age-old Persian rug making craft. On the contrary, Persian rugs, woven and then washed and sun-dried in the traditional way, are being produced and exported in greater quantities each year. Between 1963 and 1967, Iran's export of carpets has increased from $26 million to $45 million".

During a recent visit to Iran, the author saw approximately 200,000 Persian carpets in Tehran alone, not to mention the vast numbers reported to be in bank vaults as security.

One item in the favor of Oriental carpet weavers is the lack of a satisfactory substitute. Since an alternate product is not available, prices will continue to increase until the buyer's market is stablized. As long as people prosper, there will be room for luxury possessions such as Oriental carpets, either for their decorative values or investment purposes.

CARPET CHARACTERISTICS

The important characteristics that combine to form an Oriental carpet can be divided into five basic factors: pile material and construction, design and color composition, border design, foundation threads, and backing. These factors in conjunction with the carpet size and knot density determine the price of a modern Oriental carpet.

Pile Material and Construction

Knots tightly tied in a row form the pile or nap of an Oriental carpet. Wool is the universally accepted pile material for these floor coverings, yet silk, goat's hair, camel's hair, and jute are also used. A good wool carpet will generally outlast one made from the other fibers.

Wool varies according to the area where the sheep are raised — a cold, mountainous climate is conducive to good quality wool — and the mountains of Iran are known for their superior grade of wool. The long, strong fibers from the sheep's shoulders are usually selected for carpet pile material.

Silk is also used as pile material for expensive floor coverings and tapestries. Because of natural tensil strength, silk can be spun in small diameters resulting in a light weight, dense pile construction that will often exceed 1000 knots per square inch. An all silk Oriental carpet becomes not only an art piece but a piece prized by collectors. Silk carpets wear well; however, they are not abundant due to the high cost of the raw material. Initally silk was not used as a pile material in conjunction with other fibers; however, some modern Nain carpets are combining silk and wool.

Animal hair and jute piles are found only in the inexpensive tribal rugs.

Contrary to popular belief, an Oriental carpet with a thick pile is not more desirable than a thin, closely clipped one, in fact quite the opposite is ture. Superior quality wool is stronger, permitting the spinning of thinner threads which result in dense, firm, short napped carpets. Typical of these are the Nains, Isphans, and Qums.

As stated earlier, rows of knots form the basis of the Oriental carpet which is tied in three different ways. The Persian or Senneh knot is the most common and features pile threads tied around alternate warp

16

threads. See Fig. 2. Another method illustrated in Fig.2 is called the
Turkish or Ghiordes knot whereby two pile threads are tied between
two warp threads. Both the Persian and Turkish knots are acceptable. It
is difficult to differentiate between the two in a finished product,
especially a tightly woven, superior carpet.

ORIENTAL CARPET KNOT TYING METHODS

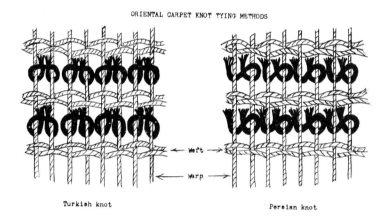

Turkish knot   Persian knot

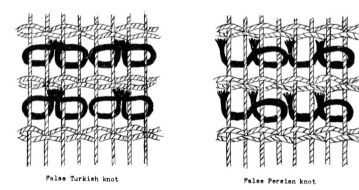

False Turkish knot   False Persian knot

Fig. 2

Another knot used to a lesser degree is the false knot or Jufti knot which features one pile thread tied on four warp threads. This method in comparison to the Persian and Turkish knot results in half the effort, half the material and time, and produces a loose, limp floor covering.

The frequency of the Persian and Turkish knots is about the same. The buyer need not worry about Jufti knots as they occur only occasionally in inexpensive carpets.

After a knot is tied, it is pulled tightly downward which directs the pile. When viewing a carpet in the direction of the pile, the carpet should appear lighter and brighter in color particularly in chemically washed rugs or silk carpets. When looking at the carpet against the pile direction, the colors will all appear darker. The pile direction can also be detected by running your fingers up and down the carpet parallel to the warp. The "smooth feel" is the direction in which the pile lays.

A wooden, comb-like instrument is used as a kneading agent to obtain a uniform, dense pile. After several rows of knots are tied, the carpet is trimmed to a desired pile thickness with special scissors. Once the carpet is completed and taken from the loom, it is again trimmed to exact specifications. See Fig. 3.

A good weaver will tie from 800 to 1000 knots per hour. The time required to complete a carpet is rather long, for example a 5' x 7' carpet exhibiting 500 knots per square inch will require slightly more than 2.5 million knots for completion. The time involved from carding the wool to the final wash can be as much as two years.

Women are often entrusted with the tedious weaving as their nimble fingers are especially capable of the intricate work of tying knots.

Design and Color Composition

Designs indigenous to specific areas will be discussed under a separate heading. Of importance here is the symmetry of the complete pattern and the intricacy of design. See Fig. 4. Designs should be as symmetrical as possible, although small mistakes or irregularities give Oriental carpets a charm of their own. More disconcerting than design faults are structural mishaps which are discussed under foundation threads. Most Oriental carpets possess a well balanced, compact design which makes them initially attractive to a buyer.

Three kinds of dyes have been used over the years in varying percentages. Initially only vegetable dyes were used, then a synthetic organic dye called analine was discovered in 1956 followed by the invention of chrome dyes. Originally red came from the roots of the madder plant and a certain few insects; yellow from reseda, sumac. and

18

Figure 3. CLIPPING A MODERN ORIENTAL CARPET After the woven carpet is taken from the loom, it is immediately clipped to a uniform size. Special scissors are used to insure an

Figure 4. MODERN DESIGN TECHNIQUES A new design is explained to the author by a master weaver in Lahore, West Pakistan. In the backround men are seated before their looms.

saffron plants; blue from the indigo plant; and gray, brown, and black from tree bark. Other colors were produced by blending the basic dyes. Natural colors were derived from the undyed animal hair.

Spun yarn is initially rinsed in a tepid water bath to which a pinch of caustic soda has been added to remove unwanted wool lanolin. The wool is then cooked in a chemical bath, dyed the desired color, and dried in the sun. See Fig. 5. In order to maintain uniform color the wool is usually processed in bulk quantities rather than in small batches.

For obvious reasons, color fastness is an important aspect of Oriental rug purchasing. Occasionally even the most reputable dealers will unknowingly possess a carpet which will fade when washed. The only safeguard is to test each carpet color by vigorously rubbing the carpet pile with a white cloth that has been emersed in warm water. Untrue colors will transfer from the rug to the cloth.

Chemical washing may not categorically come under this heading, but, since this undersirable process effects the color of Oriental carpets, the subject will be discussed in this chapter. The Iranians as well as most Europeans prefer vivid, bold colors while the American market desires subdued, pastel shades. When the American market was in its infancy, the Iranian weavers had to tone down their carpets in order to expand sales in the United States. As the American market increased in volume, lighter colored carpets were specially prepared by using a harsh, chemical wash, which bleached the bright reds and blues. This process had a detrimental effect on carpet life as it reduced the protein content of the wool, lessening its ability to stand normal wear. Later this process was altered; today rugs are lightly washed which does not materially deter the carpet life. See Fig. 6.

Border Design

Borders are difficult to weave. Patience and skill are required to properly knot the minute figures found in the border patterns of more expensive rugs. Consequently the number of borders on an Oriental carpet and individual complexities are indicative of quality.

Foundation Threads

Oriental carpets are woven on a loom which is basically a wooden structure that supports the foundation threads. See Fig. 7. The warp and weft threads are long fibrous strings that run vertically and horizontally along the loom forming the carpet foundation. Individual knots are tied on the warp threads after which the weft threads are inserted. See Fig. 2. Wool and cotton are used as foundation threads

Figure 5. PREPARING DYES Water is brought to a boil in a large kettle, and the dye is added. Yarn is piled before the kettle awaiting the dying process.

Figure 6. FINAL PROCESSING After weaving, a new carpet is washed to set the dyes. In this picture a light chemical wash is applied to the carpet to create a sheen.

Figure 7. CARPET WEAVING-LOOM. Carpet weavers sit at their loom. The various balls of colored yarn hanging overhead are used to tie the knots. This loom is one of fifty in this weaving factory.

of medium priced rugs Silk is employed in the same manner in more expensive carpets.

The longevity of a carpet is, in part, dependent upon the foundation, and a firm back will long outwear a limp back.

Goat's hair and jute are used as foundation material for inexpensive carpets, particularly tribal rugs. These materials will not last as long as wool or silk nor can they be woven into intricate designs required in Persian carpets. Jute rugs are more prevalent in India where the raw material is abundant.

Structural defects can usually be related to poor foundation material. Cheap wool warp threads may, in time, result in a "washboard" effect or a stretched carpet. Good quality wool, cotton and silk are safeguards against this adverse effect.

Backing

A hard, resilient back is an excellent criterion. A carpet exhibiting a strong underside will last longer and retain its original shape better than one having a limp back.

A proud carpet seller will invariably turn a well backed rug over and run his fingernail down the back side producing a scratchy noise. To accentuate this effect some dealers may coat the back with a clear starchy material which adds a temporary hardness. Buyers should obviously discount this effect when evaluating the underside of a carpet. The starchy back can be detected by holding the back of the carpet to the light and watching for a shiny reflection.

On the back of an Oriental carpet is one of the best places to test for machine stitching. Machine made rugs give themselves away by the continuous, exact looping of the bobbin thread on the carpet back.*

The carpet back is also the best location to discern the so called double knot in which warp threads lie at different levels. Alternate warp threads are drawn forward making half of the knot invisible from the back causing the back to become stiffer and more dense. The misnomered single knot is completely visible an appears as two double knots.

* The author visited machine made carpet shops in Pakistan and Kenya. The latter experience was interesting in that the vendor was willing to sell his 6' x 9' "Oriental carpet" for less than $100.00.

AREA DISCUSSION

Persian Carpets

The Iranian people have always exhibited a highly developed artistic craftsmanship which is evident in their carpets. These Oriental rugs are made in three distinct places, the home, the city shop, and the nomadic tent. Early Persian carpets usually reveal their site of origin because each carpet weaving area utilized designs and patterns indigenous to that area. Communication and transportation of ideas, designs, and styles from one previously isolated area to another has lessened the reliability of associating designs with areas.

Design characteristics used in Persian carpets are many, but basically only a few well known symbols are evident: stars or rosettes, palmettes or Shah Abbas designs, paisley or leaf figures, Herati patterns, and Isphan stem designs. The various plates in this book illustrate some of the more prominent design patterns used in Persian rug weaving.

Iranian carpets have been categorized in various ways. This book will treat the subject by dividing the country into eleven major areas, each area (see Fig. 1.) is a result of a prominent sales outlet. These locations are well known by Oriental carpet enthusiasts and are listed as Tabriz, Tehran, Qum, Kashan, Mashed, Kirman, Shiraz, Hamadan, Sarouk, and Nain.

For convenience, the Nomadic rugs, Turkoman and Baluchi, will be discussed under Turkoman since they are produced by migratory tribes which frequently cross country borders. To give the credit to Iran would be unfair as well as misleading.

Tabriz

Carpets sold in the Tabriz market can be sub-divided into five categories and each will be discussed individually. Tabriz carpets exhibit a short pile, the Turkish knot, and a cotton warp and weft. The newer rugs are larger, generally 7' x 10', and feature the symmetrical design of set, angular, mechanical patterns which have little appeal to the American buyer.

Koraja carpets usually appear in runner sizes, 2' x 2' to 3' x 4' and sometimes as large as 4' x 6'. This carpet utilizes a geometrical design with an occasional medallion enclosed in a field of red.

The modern Ardebil rug comes from the Tabriz district. A cotton warp and a wool nap are characteristic of these rugs which are woven in a medium dense pile of average thickness. The standard sizes are 2' x 4' to 5' x 9'. These carpets are characterized by a geometric design with a red or ivory field which is comparable to the old Caucasian designs.

The Serab rug has a thick, tightly woven pile, and more often than not is constructed of camel hair and comes mainly in runner sizes up to 3' x 4'. Usually the natural camel hair provides the color for making the eight sided Caucasian designs common to these rugs.

The Herez is the last carpet included in this group and is woven in several sizes including a 9' x 12'. Wool quality is good, and the pile is of average thickness and density. A geometric design is utilized in a field of various shades of red. Occasionally a stiff, angular floral design surrounding a large blue medallion with blue borders is woven in Herez.

Tehran

Oriental carpets made in the city of Tehran are becoming extinct. Industrialization has caused the carpet weavers to leave their poorly paying looms for more lucrative employment. Regardless of this transformation, Tehran still remains an important wholesale outlet for Iranian carpets in general.

Tehran carpets usually exhibit a short nap, above average density and come in 4' x 6' and 7' x 10' sizes. They are the least easily distinguishable of all Persian carpets as the weavers are attracted to the city from all over Iran. The Tehran carpets appear in many colors with medallions and floral sprays as well as Caucasian patterns.

Qum

Some of the finest modern rugs in Iran are currently being woven in Qum. Most of these rugs have a medium to thin pile thickness and an average knot density exceeding 300 knots per square inch. Qum carpets are woven in sizes ranging from 4' x 7' to 7' x 10' and exhibit the Persian knot. Usually the carpets have a cotton warp, but some modern, superior quality Qums have silk warp threads.

Modern Qum carpets feature traditional floral sprays in a contrasting dark background. A center medallion, overall paisley design, and set square patterns are the other characteristics peculiar to Qums.

Due to their dense construction, high quality materials, and excellent workmanship, Qum carpets sell for higher than average prices.

Kashan*

Kashan carpets utilize the Persian knot and exhibit a short, velvet-like pile woven of the finest wool. These carpets come in medium and large sizes. The average Kashan is woven with Shah Abbas rosettes or an attractive center medallion encased in an intricate floral design surrounded by a red field. Recently made Kashans display a center medallion in an open red field with delicate scrolls in the border. However some appear without a center medallion.

Isphan

Modern Isphan carpets along with Nains are probably the best woven, most expensive modern rugs produced in Iran today. They exhibit a short, dense pile with knots often exceeding 600 per square inch.

These rugs usually have a cotton warp but lately a silk warp has begun replacing cotton. The newer Isphans with a silk warp are much improved over earlier types. Almost without exception Isphan carpets have an intricate, sweeping floral design. The tendrils and stem bursts form an arabesque around a center medallion. See Fig. 9. Isphan rugs range in size from 3' x 5' to 11' x 16' and the light background generally exhibits pleasing pastel shades mixed with mild tones of red and blue.

Mashed

Mashed carpets are medium to heavy in pile thickness and possess warp and weft threads of cotton. They exhibit the Persian knot and are unique in that more often than not they are woven in square sizes. Mashed carpets are embellished with soft pastel shades employing a large, intricate, floral design outside the center medallion. Although the principal field colors are shades of red, sometimes blue is interspersed for contrast.

Masheds have long been popular in export trade due to their reasonable price and mellow colors. In recent years carpets from this area have shown a definite loss in quality.

*''In 1968 Kashan celebrates its 500th year as an important Oriental carpet making town.

28

Figure 8. DECORATIVE ARTS MUSEUM   Tehran's Decorative Arts Museum located at 227

Figure 9. IMPERIAL MOSQUE, ISPHAN, IRAN The mosque was built in 1637 near the site of an ancient caravanserai. The design on the central dome of the mosque is composed of floral tendrils and arabesques. It is from this famous religious site that the Isphan design was originally conceived.

Figure 10. CARPET WEAVING A pleasant sight in Isphan is to see a comely Iranian girl at her loom. The diagram over her head is the weaving scheme that she follows while tying the various colored knots. Usually two women are employed at each loom.

Figure 11. CARPET "AGING" Carpets are being "aged" on a roadway near Isphan. The carpets are left in the road to be run over by large trucks. This practice is seldom used, but the author feels fortunate to have photographed such unusual treatment.

Kirman

Kirman carpets, due to their desirable design and reasonable price, are some of the most popular rugs exported from Iran. They are tied with Persian knots, usually have warp and weft threads of cotton, and appear in sizes ranging from 2' x 3' to 11' x 14'. Kirmans are of medium density and possess a heavy nap.

The colors employed in Kirman medallions are usually light pastel shades in an open field of ivory, cream, or blue. The large center design stands out as a paramount feature. These Oriental carpets have a distinct Aubusson border design which is characterized by the border and field designs flowing together. Kirmans occasionally utilize inferior quality wool which illustrates a point that can't be over emphasized—the place of origin of an Oriental rug doesn't always identify it's quality. In other words, because one type of Kirman is considered an excellent carpet, it does not follow that all Kirmans exhibit the same fine craftmanship.

Shiraz

Shiraz carpets occur in many designs and qualities as well as pile densities. The number of knots can vary from 40 to 300 per square inch. Shiraz carpets are made outside the city on village looms which necessitate smaller sizes, 3' x 5', 4' x 6', 5' x 7'. It is interesting to note that carpets are brought from the villages and sold only in the main bazaar. See Fig. 12.

A distinguishing feature of the Shiraz carpet is the traditional, rectangular Caucasian design. A pear or paisley pattern surrounded by a checkerboard design within the border is typical of the modern Shiraz. These carpets are easily recognized by their wool warp, geometric pattern, and stiff back.

Hamadan

Carpets woven in Hamadan can be sub-divided into Hamadan and Sarabend. The Hamadans are by far the most important and deserve the initial discussion. These carpets are tied with a Turkish knot and the warp and weft threads can be either cotton, wool, or camel's hair. A large percentage of Hamadan rugs are woven in runner sizes ranging from 2' x 6' to 3' x 10'. They exhibit thick to heavy pile construction, coarse wool, and a density not exceeding 225 knots per square inch. The use of the geometric and Herati design in a field of red circumscribed by borders of angular vines and paisleys is typical of Hamadan carpets. Here again the Moslem weaver is influenced by the religion which surrounds him; this time it is manifested in the floral designs from the mosque at Herat.

Figure 12. TAKING RUGS TO MARKET Newly woven modern Oriental carpets are taken to the main bazaar in Shiraz, Iran. The bazaar is the only place in Shiraz where carpets can be purchased.

Turkish knots and cotton foundations are characteristic of Sarabend floor coverings. They possess a medium pile thickness with a knot density near 225 knots per square inch. These carpets are readily distinguishable by their overall flower or paisley patterns. The continuous design is usually confined within a field of red surrounded by a uniform border of conventional vines. Although the Sarabend usually has a red field, it may occasionally appear with a field of blue.

Sarouk

Prior to 1960 most Sarouk carpets bore a traditional floral pattern inscribed in a red field flanked by floral arrangements in the border. These rugs were woven with a medium dense pile consisting of 100 to 225 knots per square inch. Most of the modern Sarouk weavers concentrate on an all-over design which eliminates the significance of a center medallion. These newer Sarouks are available in a dense nap, which results in a finer carpet with a shorter pile thickness.

Sarouk carpets come in all sizes, but 4½' x 6½' are the most prevalent. The carpet's foundation threads are either cotton or wool, and the pile is tied with the Persian knot.

Sultanabad carpets, also woven in the Sarouk district, are generally large, coarsely woven, have a medium thick pile, and are considered durable. They are tied with the Turkish knot. These carpets are woven in the Shah Abbas patterns, Herati motifs, or crow-stepped medallions. Floral and stem designs dominate the red field with blue markings.

Nain

Nain carpets have an old history, but their production was interrupted from World War I until 1945. Today they approach Isphan rugs in quality and price. Medium sizes are the most common. The quality carpets have a French cotton warp tied in a thick pile exceeding 600 knots per square inch. Generally Nains have good to superior quality wool, a short nap, and more than 350 knots per square inch.

These carpets, as well as Isphans, utilize the Shah Abbas design in a field of ornate flowers, flowing vine tendrils, and short stems. Usually the background is a light cream, beige, or dark blue which accentuates the intricate floral sprays. Numerous bright shades are used for the floral arrangements, often cordoned in red and blue spray borders. During the last two years white silk has been used in pile construction to highlight the patterns. Nains are made with cotton warp threads as opposed to the silk used in Isphans.

Turkoman Carpets

Of all Oriental carpets produced today, none are as strict in conformity of pattern as the Turkoman carpets. The rugs are tied with Persian knots, the foundation threads are wool or goat's hair, and the pile varies from medium to thick. They exhibit a medium knot density not exceeding 300 knots per square inch.

The major design characteristic of a Turkoman carpet is an emblem called a "gul" or elephant's foot which can be either a four, six, or eight sided polygon. Several styles or patterns utilizing this basic design are illustrated in Fig. 13. Names for each emblem directly correspond to the tribe that first used the design.

Turkoman rugs are available in dimensions up to 5' x 8'. Larger looms are not used due to the difficulty of transporting these cumbersome devices during nomadic migrations. A few larger rugs are woven on stationary looms in Herat and Kabul, Afghanistan.

Red and black are the predominant colors. Different shades of red are dispersed within the guls while thin black or white lines are utilized to highlight the polygons. Natural dyes are still used in these areas — the red dyes come from the madder plant and the black from tree bark.

Oriental carpets featuring Turkoman designs are woven in four countries: Iran, Russia, Afghanistan, and West Pakistan. Durability, reasonable price, and simplicity of design have made these carpets world famous. The chief weavers are nomads whose main occupation is raising sheep. Almost without exception women are found working at the looms.

In the past the primary trading center for Turkoman rugs was Bokhara, Russia, which was also the intellectual center of Central Asia. Trading caravans would route their expeditions through Bokhara to purchase carpets for resale in the more lucrative western markets. Consequently, Bokhara became synonymous with Turkoman and one finds the two terms used interchangeably.

Turkoman rugs could be subdivided by countries or districts but it would require composition beyond the design of this book. In this book the reader will be provided with a short, precise description of Turkoman carpets made by the following major tribes: Tekke, Salor, Pendeh, Yomud, Afghan, and Baluchi. There are so few carpets produced by the Bokhtwari, Kurdish, Afshar, and Kashahi tribes that they do not warrant discussion.

Tekke

The Tekke tribes make their home in Russia around Ashkhabad and Merv. Some of the finest, most accurately detailed carpets of all tribal

36

Turkoman Emblem Characteristics

Tekke

Afghan

Salor

Pendeh

Baluchi

Tarantula

Figure 13

rugs are made by the Tekke weavers. Tekke carpets exhibit the principal gul pattern in three or four rows of eight sided guls joined at intersecting points by thin lines which form a rectangle. The guls are usually smaller than those found in other Turkoman designs and have contrasting color lines to accentuate individual motifs. Eight pointed stars, descriptively called tarantulas, are effectively placed in the field between the guls to add dimension and reduce monotony.

Tekke carpets are sometimes erroneously called Royal Bokhara, obviously for the sales significance of the latter name; however, there is no appreciable difference between the two.

Salor

The Salor tribe weaves a unique, eye appealing gul somewhat larger and more complicated than the Tekke design. These emblems are also eight-sided; however, they are longer on the weft side and feature angular hooks and curved edges in a stepped pattern. Three rows of alternating red medallions on a black field encased in borders of criss-crossed patterns illustrate the overall design. Usually the guls are a shade of red in a field of black. Quite often, individual emblems are highlighted with thin white or other light colored lines.

Yomud

Yomud carpets are similar to Tekke carpets, the former being less expensive. They are woven by the tribal people from northeastern Iran, western Afghanistan, and northern West Pakistan. Shades of red, occasionally approaching a rust color, are used in these rugs. A number of newer Yomud carpets utilize the eight pointed star or tarantula design for the central theme as well as using it effectively to complete the field between the Tekke guls. Borders on these carpets often reveal either large, stubby flowers, Caucasian-like geometric figures, or criss-cross patchwork.

Pendeh

The Pendeh gul is perhaps the least complicated of Turkoman designs as opposed to the intricate Salor gul. Pendeh patterns are noted for their four parallel sides in a step pattern forming a polygon. This design is woven in West Pakistan and northern Afghanistan.

Pendeh carpets possess a field of red, ivory, brown, or blue and exhibit three or four rows of guls alternating between rows of four pointed stars. The border has a zig zag pattern or small rosette sequence.

Afghan

Afghan carpets, also called Khiva carpets, have easily discernible equi-sided guls which are larger than other Turkoman guls. These closely spaced guls are quartered in contrasting colors, usually located in three or four rows and feature a diamond in the center of each gul.

Afghan rugs are made from Bokhara, Russia, to the Hindu Kush Mountains and are popular because of their hard woven nap, simple design, and reasonable price. The pile of Afghan rugs is thicker than many of the other Turkomans, appearing to have more texture and to be coarser.

Medium red shades are used in contrast to the black in the quartered gul. Very few other colors appear in these all wool rugs, thereby facilitating their easy identification. These red and black Afghans are one of the few Turkoman rugs available in large sizes.*

Baluchi

Some of the Baluchi carpets are the coarsest rugs in the Turkoman group. They appear in a wide range of bold, geometric motifs including large octagons, pine cones, eight pointed stars, and alternating rows of diamonds. Baluchis are woven along the Iran-Pakistan border and are more detailed than most Turkoman rugs. Red designs in a field of black are still prevalent, but lighter colors are now being incorporated. Border patterns are woven in either stiff stemed flowers, zig zag geometric figures or diamonds surrounding crosses.

New Baluchi carpets of natural wool are appearing in West Pakistan as a result of the government sponsored village weaving industry. Most of the looms, under this program, are located in small sparsely populated areas.

---

* One hotel in Karachi, West Pakistan, owns an Afghan measuring over 400 square feet and containing 120 guls.

Pakistani Carpets

The Pakistani Oriental carpet industry was started in 1947 but did not flourish until 1958 when the Government initiated federal support in an effort to expand export sales.* Prior to 1958 Pakistani carpets were considered on the periphery of the Oriental carpet world contributing little to the design and eventual evolution of the modern Oriental carpet.

Originally, Pakistani carpet weavers borrowed Turkoman designs from the tribal people migrating across the borders of Afghanistan, Iran, and Pakistan. Later as the weaver's skills developed, Persian designs, particularly Kirman and Kashan patterns, were added along with rudimentary Caucasian designs. Currently the Pakistan Oriental carpet industry relies heavily on Turkoman patterns with an occasional Persian and Caucasian design. Early Pakistani carpets exhibited a weak fringe; however, this defect has been altered. A soft, limp pile is a readily noticeable feature which should be overcome to increase appreciation of these carpets.

Average priced Pakistani rugs with the exception of the Mori carpets are usually tied with the Persian knot, possess either wool or cotton foundation threads, come in medium sizes, and exhibit a medium thick pile. Newer, more expensive creations utilize only cotton warp threads with a short clipped Australian wool nap.

Many private companies are engaged in carpet weaving in Pakistan not to mention the Government sponsored industries. The Government expects to increase foreign exchange earnings by exporting carpets to Western markets. Currently, the Government is turning out about 150 trained weavers per year, most in underdeveloped regions of the country.

Originally design characteristics, weavers, and construction methods were imported into Pakistan to establish their Oriental carpet industry. Methods have diameterically changed in the last decade; export as well as indigenous sales have increased through refinements in production techniques, quality control, and more accurate design characteristics.

Pakistani Oriental carpets are characterised by five basic patterns: Mori, Turkoman, Persian, Caucasian, and Prayer.

Mori

Moris are woven along the Afghan-Pakistan border, but nevertheless are classified as Pakistani. These finely woven creations compare favorably with many of the upper-middle grade Persians carpets. They

* The initial subsidy of 30-40% was discontinued in December 1967.

feature a smaller type Turkoman Tekke gul encased in a field of red, green, or light pastel shades. Mori carpets are distinguished by a Kashmiri wool nap and a dense pile exceeding 600 knots per square inch. These all wool carpets range in sizes up to 5½' x 7½' and are perhaps the most costly woven in Pakistan. Moreover Mori carpets possess a strong, hard back as opposed to the usual soft, limp underside of most Pakistani floor coverings.

Turkoman

The Pakistani carpet industry utilizes three Turkoman patterns: Tekke, Salor, and Afghan. Tekke designs are prevalent and account for approximately half of the production.

It is difficult to differentiate Pakistani made Turkomans from those made in Afghanistan and Russia because materials, design, and weaving techniques approach a common standard. One way to distinguish between the two is to "feel" the backside. Original Turkoman carpets have the hard, stiff back while the Pakistani types are soft and pliable.

Persian

Both Kirman and Kashan designs are found in Pakistani made carpets. Originally these designs were chosen as they did not demand of the weavers the intricacy and skill necessary to produce carpets like the Iranian Nains and Isphans. Nevertheless, the Pakistani woven Kirman and Kashan designs can be compared to their Persian counterparts with the exception of the limp back feature which is not conducive to long wear.

Caucasian

The fourth major Pakistani Oriental carpet is the Caucasian which incorporates the angular geometric and stiff floral patterns which made Tabriz carpets world famous. Pakistani versions feature the same bold, contrasting color schemes employed in Tabriz floor coverings.

The Pakistani produced Caucasian carpets have the typical soft, limp underside which is the only characteristic that distinguishes them from the originals.

Prayer

Due to the religious significance in the formation of Pakistan, the development of the prayer rug has had particular impetus in Pakistan. Originally, prayer type carpets were woven in Turkey, but today many are coming from Pakistan. These rugs are easy to detect as they do not exhibit symmetry around the weft axis but feature a sharp arrow-like point which must face Mecca when the Moslem prays. The pattern usually depicts a mosque as the center theme; however, Turkoman guls are also utilized to a lesser extent.

These carpets are woven in small sizes, 2' x 3', but occasionally a medium size prayer rug is found. Primarily the larger ones are used as floor decorations.

Unusual variations occur in these rugs such as the use of hands in the upper section of the carpet, birds which symbolize a closeness to Allah, and specific characteristics of the mosque, i.e. steps and minarets.

Indian Carpets

India embarked upon Oriental carpet weaving in the late 1500's by importing Persian weavers. However, India's Oriental carpet industry expanded only recently when export markets were established. The slow start in Indian rug weaving was, in part, due to the climate of the country, which does not require floor coverings to help repel cold weather. Thus, possessing no practical value, Indian carpets were only bought by the wealthy who desired them solely as a status symbol.

As Persian Oriental carpets became more costly, Indian weavers, depicting old Eruopean designs, began to sell their rugs in the export market. The trend has continued, and today India ranks second in world production of Oriental carpets, exporting primarily to Great Britain, Europe, Canada, South Africa, and the United States. Due to the sheer number of Indians employed in this industry, India may surpass Iran as the world's largest Oriental carpet producer.

India weavers turn out numerous Oriental carpet designs among the most prominent are the Sirdar, Indian-Savonnerie, Kashmir, Chinese, Turkoman, and Persian. Most of the weaving is concentrated around Amirtsar, Srinagar, Agra, and Jaipur.

Sirdar

Sirdar is not only a design but also the brand name for a durable, plain, pastel colored carpet featuring embossed borders. These hand knotted rugs exhibit one color tone of either ivory, beige, wine, or green and are woven in sizes from 2' x 4' to 12' x 20'. More over the pile of the Sirdar carpet is exceptionally thick and the all wool construction results in a durable floor covering. A loose knot density and an average count of 50 to 75 knots per square inch are responsible for the low price.

Indian-Savonnerie

Indian-Savonnerie, an early French design, features a center medallion in an open field. These carpets are not as intricate as Persian rugs but nevertheless they exhibit a regal appearance and colors similar to the Kirman. The field is either open or decorated, colored in light pastel shades, and features bold contrasting borders. Indian-Savonneries also come without a medallion, in dark blue or green fields, and are available in standard sizes from 3' x 5' to 12' x 20'. There are many trade names for these carpets among the most promient are Indian-Aubusson, Kalabar, Kandahar, and Malabar. Indian-Savonnerie carpets are desirable because of their pleasing pastel color schemes, thick durable wool pile, and reasonable price.

Kashmir

Several Oriental carpet designs are woven in Kashmir. The "Jewel of Kashmir" design is the most popular and features a dark center medallion in a light pastel field. These carpets are densely knotted; however, they feature a thin pile and possess a limp underside.

Kashmiri rugs are a favorite with the many tourists who visit this famous resort. Besides the "Jewel of Kashmir" rugs, others are found in an abundance of designs and vibrant color combinations.

Due to the fine texture of Kashmir wool, these rugs can be densely knotted resulting in a short clipped intricately designed floor covering. These rugs are steadily gaining acceptance in the export market.

Chinese

The final design that has gained poplarity among Indian Oriental rugs is the embossed Chinese pattern. They are finished by clipping around each individual pattern with special scissors which creates a sculptured effect. Two brand names are available in Chinese designs, Bengali and Chinda. The Bengali carpet is usually a combination of three pastel colors, shaded in an ivory field. These carpets feature typical Chinese designs embossed on an all wool, medium-thick nap. Bengalis are woven in standard sizes ranging up to 12' x 20'.

The Chinda is typified by a heavy, dense, all wool pile woven in standard sizes. Many designs are incorporated into Chinda carpets which feature chrome dyed yarn of standard colors. Mellow tones, durability, and reasonable prices have given these carpets a wide acceptance.

Chindas are a popular export item. The Indian government through their small industries scheme has established a system of quality control to insure uniform products for foreign markets.

Persian and Turkoman

Persian designs most copied by Indian weavers are the Kashan, Isphan, and Kirman. These carpets lack the usual Persian quality, intricacy, and hard back. They are purchased purely because of functional value and reasonable price.

Tekke and Salor guls are woven into Indian carpets in an effort to duplicate Turkoman styles. As in Persian varieties, average quality is discounted by an admissible price.

Caucasian Carpets

The area from the Black Sea to the Caspian Sea is known as the Caucasus. See Fig. 1. This land mass has come under many rulers resulting in a mixture of tongues and tribes. The Caucasus is famous for its past effort in Oriental rug weaving and consequently the various geometric design characteristics are known the world over.

A discussion of Caucasian rugs in this book is slightly academic as present production from the Caucasus is very limited; therefore, little can be said about modern Caucasian carpets. Nevertheless, the old Caucasian weavers established a style that is currently duplicated in the Ardebil section of Iran and in numerous parts of West Pakistan. These patterns, once seen, can not be mistaken for any other Oriental carpet design.

Most Caucasian carpets are woven with good quality wool and occasionally there are more than 200 knots per square inch. These rugs are tied entirely with the Turkish knot. Their basic foundation is wool, cotton is rarely used. Caucasian carpets are sold mostly in the USSR; only a few reach the United States where a custom duty of 45 percent is required compared to 22½ percent for carpets from most of the other carpet weaving countries. Prior to 1960, the Caucasus produced only a few hand knotted Oriental carpets. However, with rising prices, the Caucasus like India and Pakistan found lucrative profits by selling to the Western world. It is doubtful if a foothold will be established for Caucasian carpets in the United States where tastes are different and import duties higher.

Antique Caucasian carpets were woven in many locations throughout the Caucasus. Modern rugs are limited to more productive, state managed looms. Details, patterns, design characteristics, and weaving methods are strikingly similar; therefore, this section will deviate from past chapters by just listing the characteristics of Caucasian carpets in general and not by areas.

Caucasian Oriental carpet patterns have definite traditional tendencies that can be divided into geometric designs and stylized figures. Geometric medallions assume the shape of stars, squares, swastikas, and diamonds. Designs exemplifying animals, people, and flowers were borrowed from Perisan weavers. However, the likeness is not similar as the Caucasians feature short, stubby, straight patterns as opposed to the long flowing floral designs of Persian carpets. See Fig. 14. The borders of these carpets are depicted "S" shapes, wine cups, crabs, hexagonal latticework, and diagonal strips.

Bold, bright colors are traditionally consistent in Caucasian carpets. Red is always represented along with varying amounts of blue, yellow, ivory, brown, and green.

Several Caucasian names are famous in the Oriental carpet world: Kuba, Kazak, Derband, and Daghestan. Perhaps the design receiving the most attention today is the Shirvan which is a dense, all wool carpet featuring bold, bright colors in traditional geometric patterns.

Persian Paisley

Persian Medallion

Caucasian Paisley

Caucasian Medallion

CARPET DESIGNS

Fig. 14

Chinese Carpets*

Oriental carpet weaving was introduced into China in the Seventeenth Century. Today, modern weaving centers are located in Peking, Shanghai, and Tientsin and insist on strict, standardized production techniques.

Chinese weavers use the Persian knot. These durable carpets feature a heavy, coarse, wool pile which can be as much as two inches in thickness. Foundations are mostly wool, but cotton is used in some instances. Without exception the rugs are sparsely knotted and average about 50 knots per square inch. This last factor is the primary reason for their moderate price.

Patterns and design characteristics convey a special meaning among the Chinese, and, even though their looms were destroyed during World War II, modern Chinese carpets still adhere to the old traditions. Newer designs are also appearing which parallel European patterns.

The general design of Chinese carpets is a central medallion and corner pattern in an open field. The design can be split into two distinct categories; first, the Aubusson which is reminiscent of the regal French floral patterns made popular by Indian carpets, and, secondly, the traditional Chinese motifs depicted by lotus blossoms, wheels, drums, flutes, fans, swords, and swastikas. Composite motifs include mountains, rocks, good luck characters, and cloud banks. Taoist and Buddist emblems are also included in the latter group.

Individual designs are usually embossed by cutting and flaring the material around each design to create a sculptured effect. Embossed patterns are further highlighted by multicolor schemes including blue, rose, gold, beige, and green. Occasionally monotones are woven which effectively enhance simplicity. And significant is the fact that Chinese employ chrome dyes for color stability and carpet longevity.

A more recent modern pattern called the Peking design is finding favor among carpet buyers. This design features various strict geometric good luck symbols.

---

* Since the U.S. does not trade with China, none of these modern carpets are available in the U.S. nor are U.S. citizens allowed to import the rugs. The only present prospect of importing authentic Chinese carpets into the U.S. is from Hong Kong where a few modern Chinese rug factories are located. Purchasers must obtain a Certificate of Origin from the retail outlet before the carpet can be taken into the U.S. This certificate guarantees that the carpet was not woven in Communist China.

Turkish Carpets

Turkish Oriental carpets were first made in the Twelfth Century. At that time they were called Anatolia carpets, a name sometimes used today. These floor coverings featured stiff, geometric patterns and stylized figures. Large numbers of prayer rugs were woven for the devout Moslem who kneels and reveres his Diety five times each day. Both the standard and the prayer rugs exhibit bold colors.

Prior to 1922 the Turkish carpet industry exported many rugs to the European market; however, virtually all weaving was stopped when the new Government of Kemal Ataturk deported large numbers of Greek-Turkish citizens to Greece. Unfortunately many of these people were the chief weavers of Turkish carpets.

Today Turkey is pressing for industrialization and higher standards of living, both of which are not synonymous to carpet weaving expansion. However the Turkish Oriental carpet weaving industry is not completely relegated to the annals of history. A few floor coverings featuring the traditional designs but lacking the old Turkish charm and precision are still being produced today. A few prayer rugs are exported to Western markets, but as yet, have found little success as objects of art.

ECONOMICS OF ORIENTAL CARPET BUYING

Many Oriental carpet books treat the economics of rug buying as an exogenous factor beyond the scope of written words. Measures are needed to help carpet buyers decisively assess rugs according to existing price factors. Every publication on Oriental carpets suggests buying from reputable dealers just as books devoted to furniture, clothing, cars, etc. advise like measures. This truism certainly has merit, particularly for the neophyte. However this book offers a change from previous disquieting publications in that fundamental guidelines are presented for determining Oriental carpet prices in the country of origin.

Basic Carpet Features

The important characteristics that combine to determine Oriental rug prices can be distilled from the five basic features discussed under the chapter entitled "Carpet Characteristics". The relevant categories are 1) pile material: kind, quality, type, and texture; 2) design: composition and color scheme; 3) number and intricacy of borders; 4) foundation threads; and 5) backing. For brevity, the above basic carpet features will be called 1) pile, 2) design, 3) borders, 4) foundation, and 5) backing.

Rug Density

The number of knots per square inch or rug density is easily approximated by counting the number of knots along one inch of warp and one inch of weft. Multiply these two numbers to obtain the rug density. For example, one inch of knots along the warp amounting to 25 and one inch along the weft amounting to 20 will produce 500 knots per square inch. See Backing section.

Carpet Area

The area of a carpet can be found by multiplying in feet the carpet length by the carpet width. A rug measuring 4' x 6' has a carpet area of 24 square feet.

Carpet Factor

The cost of living, wages paid to weavers, and quality of the finished product varies in each weaving country. For example, in Iran the standard of living is high resulting in higher wages which are transferred to the carpet buyer. In Afghanistan the opposite is true resulting in lower priced rugs. Therefore a CARPET FACTOR must be assigned to each country in order to make it mathematically possible to assess the cost of an Oriental carpet.

The CARPET FACTOR for Iran and the Caucasus is the highest due to reasons stated above and varies from .020 to .025, is dependent upon the five BASIC CARPET FEATURES. Example: If the pile of a carpet is of good quality, smooth wool, and at least medium thin, allocate one point; if the carpet has an appealing, intricate design, mark a second point; if it has numerous, symmetrical, well defined borders, mark a third point; if the carpet foundation is of silk warp threads or quality cotton threads, allow a fourth point; and lastly, if the backing has a hard, resilient surface, add the fifth point. Now add the allocated points, one to five, to the basic .020 for the final factor.

Oriental carpets woven in Pakistan and India are more moderately priced than Iranian and Caucasian rugs as the cost of living, weaving skills, and wages are not as high. The CARPET FACTOR for these two countries varies between .015 and .020. The five point spread is figured in the same manner as stated in the preceding paragraph. One exception must be included at this point. Indian carpets with extremely thick piles (over one inch) and a small knot density (less than 70 knots per square inch) will invariably have a higher CARPET FACTOR than determined by the method stated. This is caused in part by equating the total amount of wool used in comparison to the amount of work involved in tying the less dense carpet.

Upon comparing the basic carpet features of the different types of Turkoman floor coverings, one finds a striking resemblance. For example their designs are basically similar, all possess wool pile and foundation material, and pile thickness and borders are virtually the same. Therefore the CARPET FACTOR for Turkomans does not vary, and, due to a less advanced standard of living, the factor is fixed at .015, the lowest of CARPET FACTORS.

Determining Carpet Cost

To find the price of a carpet simply multiply the RUG DENSITY times the CARPET AREA times the CARPET FACTOR.

Example No. 1: A hypothetical Persian carpet with three good factors:

complicated design, silk warp, and superior wool pile. Rug Density is 25 x 20 or 500 knots per square inch. Carpet Area is 4' x 6' or 24 square feet. Carpet Factor is .023. Therefore 500 x 24 x .023 equals 276 or $276.00

Example No. 2: A hypothetical Pakistani carpet with 2 plus factors: many intricate borders and excellent symmetrical design. Rug Density is 15 x 15 or 225 knots per square inch. Carpet Area is 3' x 5' or 15 square feet. Carpet Factor is .017. Therefore 225 x 15 x .017 equals 58 or $58.00

Example No. 3: A hypothetical Turkoman carpet: Rug Density is 12 x 15 or 180 knots per square inch. Carpet Area is 9' x 12' or 108 square feet. Carpet Factor is .015. Therefore 180 x 108 x .015 equals 291 or $291.00

For those readers who loath mathematical calculations, a graph has been coveniently provided to assist in determining the approximate carpet price. See Fig. 15. Use the graph in the following manner:

1. Determine the Rug Density or knots per square inch of the carpet and mark it on the left hand vertical axis of Fig. 15.
2. Move horizontally from the knot column until the correct rug size is intersected, 3' x 5' or 5' x 7', etc; interpolation may be necessary.
3. From this point, move downward to the horizontal axis and read the appropriate figure, 10,000, 20,000, etc.
4. Transpose this last reading to the right vertical axis.
5. Move left horizontally until the correct carpet factor line is intersected, .015, .020, etc.; interpolation may again be necessary.
6. Finally, move vertically to the upper horizontal axis to determine the price in U.S. dollars.

Example.

Suppose the Rug Density is 500 knots per square inch, Carpet Size is 4' x 6', and Carpet Factor is .023. Proceed horizontally to the right from 500 knots per square inch on the left vertical axis and intersect the 4' x 6' carpet size line. Drop down to the lower horizontal axis and read 12,000. Mark 12,000 on the right vertical axis and proceed to the left and intesect the .023 carpet line; interpolation is necessary. Move vertically to intersect top horizontal price line at $275.00.

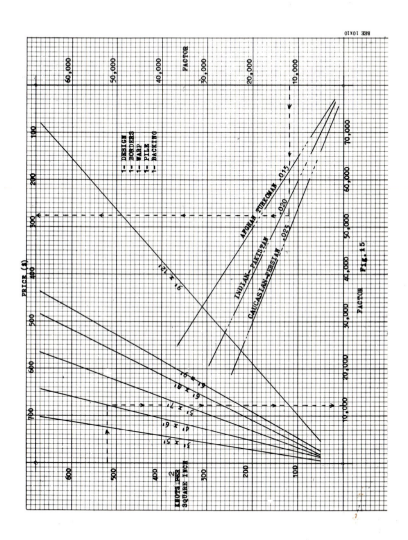

Fig. 15

Carpets purchased outside the country of manufacture are considerably more expensive because of import duties and added selling costs. The increase in price varies according to the country concerned but usually the value is increased from 2 to 2½ times the initial price. Table 1 provides a quick price reference to the various carpets illustrated in this book.

Good buys are often found at auctions and clearance sales which are generally announced in advance in leading newspapers, permitting prospective buyers to inspect the carpets prior to the sale. In either case, the buyer should be discriminating and knowledgeable as carpets cannot be subsequently returned.*

Now that buying an Oriental carpet has been discussed, a thought on selling these floor coverings is necessary. One difference between the investment prospensity of Oriental rugs and other negotiable secutities is that it takes time to dispose of carpets. People selling rugs in a hurry always receive less money than desired, so it is best to bow to the inevitable before the last moment in order to get a better deal.

* A noteworthy auctioneer is the U.S. Government in Washington D.C. who periodically auctions carpets which have been confiscated for unpaid customs duties.

Figure 16. CARPET SALE The author visits a carpet clearance sale in Lahore, West Pakistan. A prudent, knowledgeable buyer can find excellent bargains at such sales.

CARPET CARE

Oriental carpet have three principal enemies, wear, dirt, and insects. Protective measures, washing processes, and storage facilities are aimed at lessening the determinental effects caused by these three offenders. Moths and carpet beetles can ruin a carpet in a matter of days. Rugs in storage or not in use are much more susceptible to insect damage. The carpet area covered by chairs, couches, etc., result in hidden enclaves where insects naturally seek shelter. The best defence is to spray an insect repellent on your carpets every six months. Directions on the container must be followed to ensure proper application. It is important to treat each side of the rug in order to ensure maximum protection.

When storing an Oriental carpet for long periods of time, the rug should be rolled against the pile and moth balls inserted periodically during the rolling process. Carpets should be rolled because folding crushes the pile and creates crease lines which are not only noticeable but will damage the carpet's foundation and pile.

Dirt which filters down through the carpet pile and collects on the foundation is the second enemy. If not extracted, these fine, hard particles will erode the pile threads and shorten the carpet's life. Dirt can be removed by either beating, vacuuming, or washing. The former is permissible if the proper carpet beating instrument is used instead of an ordinary stick which tends to loosen knots. Carpets should always be beaten from the back side in order to force the dirt out through the pile. Another method for cleaning an Oriental carpet is the vacuum cleaner, which should be used weekly. The carpet should be vacuumed in the direction of the pile. A brush can always be used in the same manner, however, neither method is a substitute for the wash.

Numerous methods are acceptable for washing a rug. See Fig. 17 to 20. The most obvious and satisfactory is to take the carpet to a reputable cleaning house. If frugality is a factor or cleaning houses unavailable, then one must wash his own carpets. One method is to emerse the carpet in a tepid water bath using a mild industrial cleaning liquid similar to "Woolite". A bath tub is an ideal receptical because of the increased ease in "jigging" the carpet up and down to loosen the dirt. Several rinses are necessary prior to drying the carpet on a flat, level surface.

Carpet wear is the last deterimental effect to be discussed. Diametrically opposed to some thinking, Oriental carpets are susceptible to wear and eventually will wear out. See Fig. 21. In order to insure longevity several ideas are advanced. Carpets should be placed on level floors free of rough spots and away from the mainstream of

Figure 17. CARPET WASHING IN REY, IRAN A warm water outlet from an underground stream of unknown origin is located in Rey, on the outskirts of Tehran, Iran. The outlet, shown above, is used to wash many carpets each year. The claim is made that the chemicals of the water add life to carpets and fastness to colors.

Figure 18. CARPET DRYING AT REY, IRAN After the carpets are washed in Rey, Iran, they are dried in the sun. Here the author is inspecting some of the newly washed carpets.

Figure 19. CARPET DRYING IN KABUL, AFGHANISTAN This unusual method of drying carpets evenly is employed in Kabul, Afghanistan. This technique allows the carpets to dry evenly.

58

Figure 20. CARPET RINSING Liberal amounts of fresh water are applied as a final rinse. The carpet is placed on a hard, sloping surface which facilitates the rinsing process.

Figure 21. CARPET REPAIRING A young apprentice looks on as a carpet weaver extracts damaged threads which will be matched for color and rewoven to the correct density.

traffic. Turned over edges caused by new, tightly woven carpets, should be corrected by sewing cardboard or leather strips to the back side until the carpet lies flat. Whenever furniture rests on carpets, furniture protectors should be inserted between the legs and the carpet surface.

Poor wool or cotton rugs that have stretched warp threads will appear bumpy or like a washboard. Quite often this defect can be corrected by stretching the carpet in the following manner: tie both carpet warp fringes in many places to separate rigid bars. Hang the carpet up at one end and add weight to the free bar at the lower end. Apply a thin coat of water to the back side of the carpet. The rug should be completely dry before removing the stretching aids. This method will not work on rugs possessing silk threads as silk has intrinsic tensil strength inhibiting the process.

Finally, several "don'ts" to keep in mind:
1. Don't wash an Oriental carpet too often.
2. Don't lay carpets on uneven floors.
3. Don't beat carpets with a stick.
4. Don't use a harsh soap.
5. Don't fold carpets for prolonged storage.

MODERN
ORIENTAL
CARPETS

PLATE NO. 1

TABRIZ

This Tabriz carpet portrays a geometric, stylized flower pattern. The carpet has a thick rugged pile. Foundation threads are wool and the backing is stiff.

Pricing Factors:

200 knots per square inch, 3.2' x 5.3', wool foundation. Carpet factor points given for design, pile, and backing. Use .023 rug curve (Fig. 15) to compute a price of $78.

PLATE NO. 2

TABRIZ

Geometric designs featuring concentric diamonds and stylized flowers are common in Tabriz floor coverings. Modern Tabriz carpets do not utilize the bold colors found in older rugs. This carpet is constructed of all wool materials, a medium thick pile, and a stiff back.

Pricing Factors:

225 knots per square inch, 5.3' x 7.4', wool foundation. Carpet factor points given for design, pile and backing. The .023 rug curve of Fig. 15 indicates $203 would be a favorable price in the Tabriz district.

PLATE NO. 3

TEHRAN

Due to Tehran's composite population, carpets are woven in many different designs. This particular pattern is similiar to a Nain but not nearly as intricate in design or knot density. Both the weft and pile are of good quality wool. The nap is medium and the back is stiff.

Pricing Factors:

250 knots per square inch, 5.7' x 7.8', cotton warp. Carpet points are given for design, pile, borders, and backing. An additional point could be given for the cotton warp. Use .024 rug curve of Fig. 15 for determining the price of $270. If .025 is used, then the price would be $285.

PLATE NO. 4

TEHRAN

This carpet is basically a Sarouk design. The over-all floral and short stem pattern which omits the center medallion is typically Sarouk. The carpet has an average pile thickness and the back is hard. The warp is cotton and the weft is wool.

Pricing Factors:

320 knots per square inch, 4.8' x 6.9', cotton warp. Carpet points are given for design, pile, borders, and backing. Use the .024 rug curve of Fig. 15 to find the Tehran price of $256.

PLATE NO. 5

QUM

Oriental carpets woven in Qum are some of the finest produced in Iran today. As a result of the unsymetrical nature of the design, this Qum could qualify as a prayer rug, although it is not as definitive as most prayer rugs. This rug has a strong back, dense knot construction, and thin pile. The foundation has a cotton warp.

Pricing Factors:

520 knots per square inch, 3.5' x 5.2', cotton warp. Carpet factor points are given for design, borders, pile, and backing. Use .024 rug curve of Fig. 15 to give price of $220 if purchased in Qum

PLATE NO. 6

QUM

Qum rugs are tightly woven, well designed, and exhibit an intricate, contrasting border. Dark fields of the modern Qum carpets produce an eye pleasing effect. This carpet features a thin nap, a hard back and a quality cotton warp.

Pricing Factors:

580 knots per square inch, 5.5' x 7.8', Carpet points given for design, borders, foundation, pile, and backing. Use .025 rug curve of Fig. 15 to give the Qum price of $624.

PLATE NO. 7

KASHAN

Flower and stem designs surrounding a center medallion are typical of Kashan carpets. Usually red is the dominant color in these carpets. The total color effect of this carpet causes it to appear pale or anemic. From a distance, the carpet appears reversible as the tightly knotted and thin piled back creates the impression that the design is as bold and vivid as the face. This carpet is dense, tightly woven, and exhibits a short clipped, excellent wool pile. The turned in corners are indicative of the extremely tight weave.

Pricing Factors:

625 knots per square inch, 5' x 7', cotton warp. Carpet points given for border, pile, and backing. Use .023 rug curve (Fig. 15) to give the price of $506 in Kashan.

PLATE NO. 8

KASHAN

Kashan carpets featuring red center medallions encased in white fields are common among the modern ones made in Kashan. The back of this particular rug is not resilient but the pile is nevertheless short. Cotton is used in the foundation and the knot density is slightly less than is employed in most modern Kashans.

Pricing Factors:

350 knots per square inch, 5.3' x 7.1', cotton warp. Carpet points given for design, borders, and pile. Use .023 rug curve of Fig. 15 to determine the Kashan price of $306.

PLATE NO. 9

ISPHAN

The tendril and arabesque pattern is a trademark of Isphan carpets. This design is varied in many ground colors; the most common are pastel shades. Silk warp threads and fine cotton weft threads are evident. The design is intricate, the wool quality is excellent, and the back is hard and tight. All these characteristics combine to permit this Isphan carpet to be short clipped.

Pricing Factors:

625 knots per square inch, 4.9' x 6.9', silk and cotton foundation. Carpet factor points given for pile, design, foundation, borders, and backing. Use .025 rug curve to give the price of $527. The carpet belongs to the collection of the author and was purchased in Tehran, Iran, in December 1965.

PLATE NO. 10

ISPHAN

This modern Isphan carpet deviates from the traditional patterns in that the borders are irregular. This popular new design won an Iranian award in 1967 and proudly exhibits the weaver's name on the lower fringe. The thin tendril and arabesque are typically Isphan copied from the design of the Great Mosque in Isphan. See Fig. 9. The short clipped pile is composed of excellent wool. Silk is employed in the warp, cotton in the weft, and the back is hard and stiff.

Pricing Factors:

1040 knots per square inch, 3.2' x 5.3', silk and cotton foundation. Carpet factor points given for pile, design, foundation, borders and backing. Use .025 rug curve from Fig. 15 to give price of $443. This rug is part of the author's collection and was purchased in Isphan, Iran, in December, 1967.

PLATE NO. 11

ISPHAN

Due to the short stem and tendril arabesque pattern this Isphan carpet is strikingly similar in design to a Nain. However, the weaver's name woven in the bottom fringe states, "made in Isphan, Iran". The design is not as intricate as Plate No. 9. The closely clipped wool pile is of excellent quality. Foundation materials are silk and cotton. The back is hard and resilient.

Pricing Factors:

625 knots per square inch, 4.8' x 6.9', silk warp and cotton weft. Carpet factor points given for pile, design, foundation, borders, and backing. Use .025 rug curve to approximate a price of $518. This rug was purchased by the author in Tehran, Iran, in December 1965.

PLATE NO. 12

KIRMAN

Through the years the design of the modern Kirman has changed very little. The traditional, elongated center medallion in a solid field makes the Kirman easy to distinguish. The knot density is considerably less and as such is noticeable by the limited number of warp threads. Also the backing is limp and the pile depth is medium thick. Kirman carpets are woven in large sizes which make them suitable for dining and living rooms.

Pricing Factors:

180 knots per square inch, 6.8' x 9.5', wool foundation. Carpet points given for border. Use .021 rug curve from Fig. 15 to give the Kirman price of $243.

PLATE NO. 13

KIRMAN

Quite often white highlighting is employed in Kirman carpets. Usually the intricate corner designs will cut into the borders as is the case with this particular rug. The backing is soft and the pile is medium thick. The carpet is constructed of all wool materials but the knot density is below average.

Pricing Factors:

195 knots per square inch, 9' x 12', wool foundation. Carpet factor points given for border. Use .021 rug curve from Fig. 15 to arrive at the price of $444 if purchased in Kirman.

PLATE NO. 14

SHIRAZ

Modern Oriental carpets from the Shiraz district are woven from hard, coarse materials resulting in a rugged, durable floor covering. This particular geometric patterned carpet has been lying at the main entrance to the hotel located at the ruins in Persepolis, Iran. This hotel has at least three such carpets in each room. All were reported to have been purchased in early 1962 and appear to be in excellent condition. Modern Shiraz carpets deviate little from past designs which employed nomadic patterns. A very tough goat's hair binding is employed in the selvages. The pile and warp are coarse wool; the density is usually loose.

Pricing Factors:

150 knots per square inch, 3.4' x 5.2', wool warp. Carpet factor points given for backing. Use .021 rug curve to indicate Shiraz price of $56.

PLATE NO. 15

SHIRAZ

This modern Shiraz carpet, as compared to Plate No. 14, creates a more eye appealing, richer appearance which results from the softer color scheme and modern geometric design. Carpets of this type are finding buyers in Tehran and the Western world. The knot density is a little tighter, the design is more complicated, and the pile is a better quality wool. All these factors combine to make this carpet more expensive when compared to the similar size and characteristics of the rug illustrated in Plate No. 14.

Pricing Factors:

210 knots per square inch, 3.4' x 5.2', wool foundation. Carpet points given for design, pile, and backing. Use .023 rug curve of Fig. 15 to arrive at price of $84 if purchased in the main bazzar in Shiraz.

PLATE NO. 16

HAMADAN

The town of Hamadan is the center of a large carpet weaving area; thus many different designs and qualities are produced in surrounding villages. Some carpets, similar to the one illustrated, are geometric in design exhibiting excellent qualities and workmanship. More modern Hamadans, employing geometric designs, utilize softer color schemes such as blue and buff combinations. This carpet is proportionately longer than other Persian rugs which makes it suitable for hallways. Of particular notice is short clipped wool pile, the average knot density, and the all wool foundation.

Pricing Factors:

285 knots per square inch, 4.5' x 6.9', wool warp. Carpet factor points given for design, pile, and backing. Use .023 rug curve to give a favorable Hamadan price of $212.

PLATE NO. 17

HAMADAN

This geometric designed carpet comes from the Saraband section of Hamadan. It was photographed by the author who saw it hanging outside a carpet store in Quetta, West Pakistan. The knot density is less than average but the thick pile is of good quality wool. This rug does not possess the hard, rugged back that is common among most Persian carpets.

Pricing Factors:

190 knots per square inch, 5.5' x 7.4', wool warp. Carpet factor points given for design. Use .021 rug curve to give possible purchase price in Hamadan of $163.

PLATE NO. 18

SAROUK

The materials used in this Sarouk are of excellent quality. The floral spray design and dark background are common in Sarouk carpets. An all-over design, as opposed to the medallion design, is gaining prominence in modern Sarouk carpets. Many such designs, as illustrated in this plate, are available in leading Iranian stores. The knot density is high, the warp is of excellent cotton, and the pile is thin. In addition the carpet exhibits a hard, resilient back.

Pricing Factors:

410 knots per square inch, 4.9' x 6.7', cotton foundation. Carpet factor points given for design, borders, foundation, pile and backing. Use .025 rug curve of Fig. 15 to give a reasonable price of $336 if purchased in the Sarouk area.

PLATE NO. 19

SAROUK

This carpet is of lesser quality than the one illustrated in Plate No. 17. By contrast the design is not as intricate or complicated as the previous Sarouk. The foundation is also constructed of lesser quality materials. Nevertheless, the geometric design of concentric diamonds presents an appealing pattern. The pile is medium thick due to the coarse wool used in the pile construction. Knot density is only average and the back is slightly limp.

Pricing Factors:

225 knots per square inch, 4.2' x 5.4', wool materials. No carpet factor points are given in this illustration, although possibly one could be given for the backing. Use .020 rug curve for a price of $104, however if one point is given for backing, then use .021 rug curve from Fig. 15 to arrive at price of $108.

PLATE NO. 20

NAIN

This modern Nain carpet features white silk highlighting throughout the design. The main medallion, floral sprays, and border design are embellished by parallel silk lines that are slightly embossed to reflect the light. A spot light can be used to bring out the color effect when such an artistic piece is hung and used as a tapestry. The pile is thin and is constructed with wool and silk. The center medallion and short stem floral design is typically Nain. The foundation is excellent quality cotton which permits the weaving of a dense floor covering.

Pricing Factors:

785 knots density, 3.9' x 5.9', silk, wool, and cotton materials. Carpet factor points given for design, pile, foundation, borders, and backing. Three extra points are allotted to compensate for the small amount of silk used in the pile. Therefore use .028 rug curve to obtain a price of $507. This rug was purchased by the author in Tehran, Iran, in December 1967.

PLATE NO. 21

TURKOMAN

Pictured is a traditional Turkoman carpet featuring the Tekke pattern. These carpets are woven by the Tekke tribe and exhibit the small Tekke gul in a dark ground color. Rugs employing brown fields as well as other non-black colors are experiencing wider sales in export markets. Hour-glasses and stylised flowers are employed in the numerous borders. The knot density of this illustration is exceptionally high and the foundation is good quality wool. The thin pile has a resilient back which makes this particular carpet a long lasting hard wearing floor covering.

Pricing Factors:

580 knots per square inch, 5.6' x 7.9', wool materials. Use .015 rug curve which is standard for Turkoman carpets to arrive at price of $386 if purchased in the Turkoman area.

PLATE NO. 22

TURKOMAN

This carpet was woven by the Salor tribe and illustrates the Salor gul alternating in a dark field. Good quality wool is used in the pile and foundation permitting a thin, rugged floor covering. The back is hard, and the knot density is above average. The design and color scheme exhibited in this plate are typical of Salor carpets which have not materially changed over the years.

Pricing Factors:

420 knots per square inch, 4.5' x 6.3', wool materials. Use .015 rug curve of Fig. 15 to arrive at price of $178. The rug is in the collection of the author and was purchased for the above amount in Kabul, Afghanistan, in November 1966.

PLATE NO. 23

TURKOMAN

The Pendeh gul is featured in this Turkoman carpet which employs a center row of Tarantulas to add depth to the main theme. Due to the uncomplicated nature of the Pendeh gul, some intermediate characters, such as tarantulas are required to break up the otherwise dull pattern. Knot density is average and the pile is thick. The back of this carpet is rather limp and the foundation employs wool materials.

Pricing Factors:

187 knots per square inch, 4.3′ x 6.2′, wool warp. Use .015 rug curve to give price of $75 if purchased in the Turkoman area.

PLATE NO. 24

TURKOMAN

The Afghan gul is depicted in this plate. The two color scheme of red and black is synonymous with the Afghan carpet. These carpets always exhibit a thick pile, loose knot density, and wool foundation threads. They are moderately priced resulting in a great demand for the larger sizes. The rugged materials used in weaving produce a hard wearing floor covering.

Pricing Factors:

143 knots per square inch, 9.4' x 12.6', wool warp. Use .015 rug curve to arrive at a reasonable price of $256.

PLATE NO. 25

TURKOMAN

One of many Baluchi designs is featured in this bright but not ostentatious Turkoman carpet. Many Baluchi creations utilize such color arrays, producing vivid patterns for sales appeal to foreigners as well as the nationals of Iran and Afghanistan. This carpet exhibits a thick pile and a limp back. The knot density is below average and the foundation is coarse wool.

Pricing Factors:

150 knots per square inch, 4.7' x 6.5' wool materials. Use .015 rug curve to give price in the weaving area of $69.

PLATE NO. 26

PAKISTAN

This Oriental carpet is woven by the Mori tribe which migrates across the Pakistan-Afghanistan border. The Moris will usually employ the Tekke gul and always utilize Kashmiri wool for a short clipped pile on a wool foundation. Knot density is always high in Mori carpets. Due to the construction methods, pile materials, and knot density, the Mori is perhaps the most expensive carpet woven in the Pak-Afghanistan area.

Pricing Factors:

625 knots per square inch, 4.7' x 5.9', excellent wool warp. Carpet factor points can be allotted for design, borders, pile, and backing. Use .019 rug curve to give purchase price of $330. This carpet was purchased by the author in Kabul, Afghanistan, in November 1966.

PLATE NO. 27

PAKISTAN

This plate represents a typical Ardebil carpet woven in West Pakistan. The Ardebil design is perhaps the most copied of all persian patterns due to the well known Ardebil that hangs in the Victoria and Albert Museum in London. The pile is of good quality wool and the knot density is above average but the back is limp, a characteristic of Pakistani carpets.

Pricing Factors:

350 knots per square inch, 4.9' x 6.8', cotton warp. Carpet factor points given for design, borders, warp, and pile. Use .019 rug curve of Fig. 15 to arrive at Pakistani price of $220.

PLATE NO. 28

PAKISTAN

Pictured is a modern Pakistani carpet created by the newly developed Government sponsored cottage industry program. Weavers are trained by the Government and then hired by one of the many private carpet weaving companies. A multitude of colorful, original design characteristics are available in these carpets which have caused expanding local sales because of their inexpensive price. The carpets are very loosely knotted, possess wool foundation material, and exhibit a thick pile. The back is limp.

Pricing Factors:

48 knots per square inch, 5.6' x 7.8' wool materials. No carpet factor points are given for this rug. Use .015 rug curve to arrive at a reasonable price of $32.

PLATE NO. 29

PAKISTAN

This modern Pakistan carpet has a design of its own. The colorful roses centered within the diamond shaped medallion are elevated from the rest of the patterns. The design is compact and accurate and the carpet pile is medium thick and contains a good quality wool. The foundation is cotton and the back is rather soft. The knot density is above average for Pakistani floor coverings. Carpets of this type are best employed as a wall hanging due to their very light colors and embossed characteristics.

Pricing Factors:

400 knots per square inch, 5' x 7', cotton warp and wool weft. Carpet factor points are given for design, borders, and pile. Use .018 rug curve from Fig. 15 to arrive at a reasonable price of $250 if purchased in Pakistan.

PLATE NO. 30

PAKISTAN

The Katchli prayer design, as illustrated in this plate, has been copies by numerous Oriental carpet weaving countries. This particular rug was woven near the Pakistan-Afghanistan border by the migrating Katchli tribe. Such prayer type carpets are important to the nomadic Muslims who use the rugs in their daily prayers. The knot density is tight and the pile is thin resulting in a light, durable floor covering. Foundation and pile material are wool. The back is limp and the pile is short-clipped which results in a light weight rug suitable for transportation by the nomadic tribes.

Pricing Factors:

225 knots per square inch, 4.6' x 6.4' wool construction materials. Carpet factor points given for design, borders, and pile. Use .018 rug curve to obtain a local price of $120.

PLATE NO. 31

INDIAN

Modern Indian carpet weavers are adept at copying foreign designs. The plate illustrates a Salor Turkoman design that was woven in Amritsar, India. Indian copies appear similar in design to the originals but on close inspection, the Indian rugs lack the hard, resilient backing. India carpets often feature a bolder color scheme than found in original Turkomans. The foundation is all wool, and the thick pile is loosely knotted.

Pricing Factors:

178 knots per square inch, 5.5' x 7.8' wool warp and weft. Carpet factor points given for borders, and design. Use .017 rug curve to obtain a price of $130 if purchased in India.

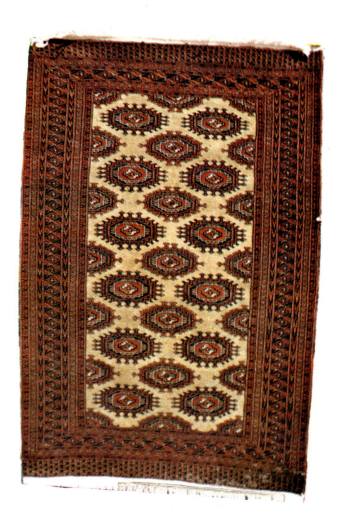

PLATE NO. 32

INDIAN

The carpet weaving industry located in Kashmir is producing many varieties of Oriental carpets. The illustrated rug, a favorite among locals and foreigners alike, is called "the Jewel of Kashmir". Neutral tones and a center medallion are characteristic of these floor coverings. Knot density is above average, foundation materials are wool, pile is thick, and backing is soft. Kashmiri carpets usually exhibit intricate designs with well developed borders.

Pricing Factors:

320 knots per square inch, 4.8' x 6.7' wool warp. Carpet factor points given for design, borders, and pile. Use .018 rug curve to obtain price of $185.

PLATE NO. 33

INDIAN

Chinese designs with circular floral patterns in a pastel field are popular among the Indian Oriental carpet weavers. The pile is exceptionally thick, the density sparse, and the back soft. An embossed floral design presents a sculptured effect. Many such designs are available from India and buyers find the soft colors and moderate prices attractive. These rugs come in various shapes, i.e., squares, rectangles, and ovals.

Pricing Factors:

75 knots per square inch, 5.2' x 7.3', very thick pile, all wool materials. Due to reasons previously mentioned under the Chinese area discussion, Fig. 15 can not be employed to determine the carpet price. However, the carpet can be purchased in India for approximately $70.

PLATE NO. 34

CAUCASIAN

Geometric designs are protrayed in Caucasian floor coverings. Quite often a three section main medallion is employed. Because of appeal gained through export the less vivid color tones are more predominant in the modern Caucasians. Stylized flowers are commonly featured to highlight various polygons in the central theme. This carpet exhibits all wool construction and is intricately designed. The borders are well woven, the back is hard, and the pile is thick.

Pricing Factors:

225 knots per square inch, 3.9' x 7.8', wool construction materials. Carpet factor points given for design, borders, pile and backing. Use .024 rug curve to get price of $164.

PLATE NO. 35

CAUCASIAN

Caucasian Carpets occasionally employ a slightly different, off center design which adds to the carpet's conversation value. In this particular case, the design of each center piece is uneven. The three piece center medallion makes the carpet appear to be much longer than it really is. This hard wearing floor covering is constructed of all wool materials which are common among modern Caucasian Oriental carpets. The pile is medium thick, the knot density average and the back hard. The foundation is wool.

Pricing Factors:

240 knots per square inch, 3.8' x 7.9', wool warp and weft. Carpet factor points given for pile and backing. Use .022 rug curve of Fig. 15 to determine the approximate price of $158 if purchased in the Caucasus.

PLATE NO. 36

CAUCASIAN

This modern Caucasian carpet features a different design from the usual employed geometric shapes. Alternate rows of acorns provide the all over pattern. Also this carpet is intricate in design, possesses good quality wool and cotton foundations, and has a closely clipped pile of excellent quality wool. The back of this Caucasian, like most of the carpets from this area, exhibits a hard, tough surface. Knot density is average.

Pricing Factors:

225 knots per square inch, 4.5' x 6.7', cotton warp and wool weft. Carpet factor points allotted for design, borders, pile, foundation, and backing. Use .025 rug curve of Fig. 15 to determine at the Caucasian price of $163.

PLATE NO. 37

CHINESE

Chinese carpets employ simple emblems in a contrasting field. Blue colors are common among these modern rugs as is the open field. This particular carpet has a very thick pile as well as an extremely small knot density; both characteristics are hallmarks of traditional Chinese weaving tendencies. The foundation and pile are woven from excellent quality wool and chrome dyes are employed to give color fastness and durability.

Pricing Factors:

80 knots per square inch, 5' x 8', all wool construction materials. This rug presents an exception to the general carpet factor formula as indicated under the area discussion. The price of this particular rug is $177 if purchased in Hong Kong.

PLATE NO. 38
CHINESE

The pictured carpet illustrates the famous Peking design; it was woven in Hong Kong. "Good luck" symbols appear at each corner in the border. These carpets can be purchased in many different ground colors. Light, pastel shades are a favorite as well as the light beige which is featured in this plate. Wool is universally used for pile and foundation materials. The pile is very thick and the knot density is less than one hundred.

Pricing Factors:

90 knots per square inch, 4' x 7', wool construction materials. As stated under the area discussion, the general price formula does not apply to these dense pile, sparsely knotted carpets.

Table One

PRICING INFORMATION

Plate No.	Area	Size Ft.	Knot Density	Pile Thickness	Pile	Carpet Design	Factor Points Foundation	Borders	Back	Price Local	Price U.S.
1	Tabriz	3.2 x 5.3	200	Medium	x	x			x	78	156
2	Tabriz	5.3 x 7.4	225	Med-thick	x	x			x	203	425
3	Tehran	5.7 x 7.8	250	Med-thick	x	x	x	x	x	285	645
4	Tehran	4.8 x 6.9	320	Med-thick	x	x		x	x	256	595
5	Qum	3.5 x 5.2	520	Thin	x	x		x	x	227	490
6	Qum	5.5 x 7.8	580	Thin	x	x	x	x	x	624	1530
7	Kashan	5 x 7	625	Thin	x	x		x	x	506	1210
8	Kashan	5.3 x 7.1	350	Med-thin	x	x		x		306	720
9	Isphan	4.9 x 6.9	625	Thin	x	x	x	x	x	527	1320
10	Isphan	3.2 x 5.3	1040	Thin	x	x	x	x	x	443	1120
11	Isphan	4.8 x 6.9	625	Thin	x	x	x	x	x	518	1290
12	Kirman	6.8 x 9.5	180	Med-thin				x		243	510
13	Kirman	9 x12	195	Med-thick				x		144	310
14	Shiraz	3.4 x 5.2	150	Med-thick					x	56	118
15	Shiraz	3.4 x 5.2	210	Medium	x	x			x	84	175
16	Hamadan	4.5 x 6.9	285	Med-thin	x	x			x	212	440
17	Hamadan	5.5 x 7.4	190	Med-thick						163	356
18	Sarouk	4.9 x 6.7	410	Thin	x	x	x	x	x	336	810
19	Sarouk	4.2 x 5.4	225	Med-thick						104	212
20	Nain	3.9 x 5.9	785	Thin	x	x	x	x	x	507	1270
21	Turkoman	5.6 x 7.9	580	Thin						386	845
22	Turkoman	4.5 x 6.3	420	Thin						178	394
23	Turkoman	4.3 x 6.2	187	Thick						75	154
24	Turkoman	9.4 x 12.6	143	Thick						256	552
25	Turkoman	4.7 x 6.5	150	Thick						69	145
26	Pakistan	4.7 x 5.9	625	Thin	x	x		x	x	330	750
27	Pakistan	4.9 x 6.8	350	Medium	x	x	x	x		220	450
28	Pakistan	5.6 x 7.8	48	Thick						32	60
29	Pakistan	5 x 7	400	Medium	x	x		x		250	500
30	Pakistan	4.6 x 6.4	225	Thin	x	x		x		120	260
31	India	5.5 x 7.8	178	Thick				x		130	260
32	India	4.8 x 6.7	320	Thick				x		185	410
33	India	5.2 x 7.3	15	Thick	x	x				70	140
34	Caucasian	3.9 x 7.8	225	Thick	x	x		x	x	164	370
35	Caucasian	3.8 x 7.9	240	Medium	x	x			x	158	340
36	Caucasian	4.5 x 6.7	225	Thin	x	x	x		x	170	355
37	Chinese	5 x 8	80	Thick	x					177	532
		5 x 7	95	Thick	x					141	423

BIBLIOGRAPHY

Igraz Schosser, BOOKS ON RUGS-ORIENTAL AND EUROPEAN, Crown, 1962.

P. Liebetrau, ORIENTAL RUGS IN COLOR, Macmillan, 1962.

Hasain, Klinkhardt & Burman, ORIENTAL CARPETS, Germany, 1963.

J.M. Con, CARPETS FROM THE ORIENT, Merlin, London, 1966.

A.C. Edwards, THE PERSIAN CARPETS, London, 1953.

C.W. Jacobsen, ORIENTAL RUGS A COMPLETE GUIDE, Tuttle, Vermont, 1962.

A.V. Dilley, ORIENTAL RUGS AND CARPETS, Scriber & Son, New York, 1913.

W.A. Hawley, ORIENTAL RUGS-ANTIQUE AND MODERN, Lane Co. New York, 1913.